Nantucket Island

Nantucket Island

Robert Gambee

Hastings House, Publishers • New York

For Mimi & Dwight Beman
and for Scott Anderson

Library of Congress Cataloging in Publication Data

Gambee, Robert.
Nantucket Island.

Bibliography
1. Nantucket, Mass.—Description and travel—Views.
I. Title.
F72.N2G17   917.44'97   73-5644
ISBN 0-8038-5058-1

Printed in the United States of America
by Rapoport Printing Corp., New York, N.Y.

Photographic consultation:

Peter C. Bunnel, Princeton University

Designed by Jacqueline Schuman

Introduction

I first saw these pictures on a day in winter when, for reasons that are now obscure, I found myself in New York City. I looked at the Queen Anne's lace by the Mill, and I saw the ponds and moors and houses and streets, and I said, "What am I doing here?" and got up and came home.

Nantucket is, quite literally, home to me, but it is also home to any number of people who aren't year-round residents. It is home to some who haven't been there for years; it is home to others who come and go with the seasons; and it is home to a great many more who, probably without knowing it, are groping for what Nantucket has to offer. It is, more than anything else, a state of mind, and those who can achieve it never want for anything more. I have written so much about Nantucket, both in fact and in fiction, that I am no longer aware of the difference between the two; Nantucket creeps into almost everything I put on paper. This is probably not a good thing, because if I were to write, say, about the Gobi Desert, it would be jarring to run across rose-covered cottages instead of camel caravans—or whatever they have in the Gobi Desert. But that's the way it is, and it's too late to change me now.

All I can do is pray that this state of mind is not obliterated by a more modern syndrome—the mindless urge to grab the fast dollar—because that, and only that, can destroy the meaning and the beauty behind these pictures.

Nathaniel Benchley

Foreword

The purpose of the Nantucket Conservation Foundation is "to promote the interest of the Town of Nantucket and its inhabitants and to assist in the preservation of its charter —

"by the conservation, preservation and maintenance of areas of beach, marshlands, meadows, wetlands . . . and greenbelt and other open areas and the animal and plantlife therein, buildings and sites of historical significance, areas of archeological or geological or other scientific significance, areas of natural beauty and areas for the conservation of public water resources . . .

"by promoting and encouraging the enjoyment and study of plants, animals, birds, and other wildlife in their natural surroundings and the study of the political, social, economic and natural history of the area . . ."

Mr. Gambee's book, through text and pictures, brings special meaning to several of the Foundation's broad field of conservation goals.

We welcome this volume and invite the reader's support of the Foundation's program to preserve for this and future generations as much as possible of the "Far-away-Island's" unique charm.

Roy E. Larsen
President
Nantucket Conservation Foundation, Inc.

Nantucket Island

1
The Forgotten Island

Have you ever been to Nantucket? And when you got home did your friends ask you how you enjoyed the Cape? Or maybe they told you about a relative of theirs who used to spend the summer on the Vineyard too.

It's interesting how little known Nantucket really is. Yet one of its greatest treasures is its isolation. Being just a little further away and harder to get to has protected it over the years. While this book seeks to portray the island as it appears today, one can never forget the tremendous history which it enjoyed—unique in many ways from all other communities in America.

For this was an island that was once, and for almost a hundred years held the honor of being, the greatest whaling center in the world (surpassing even England who long ruled the waves). It was one of the most populous communities in the early days of our country and even was described as a "city at sea" by Daniel Webster in 1835. No other town in America today has as many homes (over eight hundred) built in the period of 1740 to 1840, almost all of which are located in their original setting. During a hundred-year span, Orange Street was the home of over 125 whaling captains—a record of any such port in the country. At its peak, there were eighty-eight Nantucket whalers sailing around the world, often on voyages lasting two years or more. In fact its only major bank, established in 1804, was appropriately named the Pacific Bank, not the New England or even the Atlantic Bank.

But then came the decline, and rapid it was. It began with the Great Fire in 1846, which eliminated a third of the town and, more important, vast stores of whale oil and related items in the warehouses. The California Gold Rush siphoned off many able bodied sailors as did the Civil War. When the shifting sands made the harbor entrance unnavigable, things looked bad enough. But the discovery of petroleum and its refinement into kerosene put an end to the need for whale oil and the island's only major economy.

So rapid was the decline that by 1870 the town was an empty shell. Houses had no market value; no taxes were collected; and the island was badly in debt. The population was about a third of what it had been thirty years before. In retrospect it is fortunate that the decline was so swift and thorough. For the island was unable to experience even a small measure of the industrial revolution and the accompanying Victorian architecture that swept across the mainland.

Now, much like Brigadoon, the island has returned off the coast of America after an absence of almost a hundred years. It has come back intact (with some changes naturally) waiting to be discovered again.

Nantucket harbor from Old North Church—the
afternoon boat is just arriving from America

Great Point Lighthouse (1818), replacing the original structure built in 1784

The view of the harbor from
Monomoy

The "Nobska" rounding
Brant Point, site of the sec-
ond lighthouse built in
North America (1746) after
Boston's Beacon Light

Rainbow for hire

Fishing craft at Straight Wharf

Grand Canal

Foggy Noon

2
Why the Island Should be Remembered

The history of Nantucket is a play in three acts, each ending with a major climax—the American War of Independence, the War of 1812 and the grand finale of the late 1840's. There were other setbacks along the road, of course, mostly connected with whaling. And whaling was Nantucket's economy. Two additional factors were important contributors to the program: the Quaker religion and isolation. Without these three elements an entirely different history might have evolved. As it was, Quakerism provided the simple faith and stability that enabled Nantucketers to survive the whaling difficulties. The tenets of the religion were basic and therefore appealing to a rather simple, hard working, but extremely isolated, society.

The importance of whaling to Nantucket has already been mentioned. In fact, they were almost forced into it because there were no other resources on the island. The land was sandy, had no wood to speak of and was filled with hills, marshes and swamps. Farming and sheep husbandry were tried (the sheep population in 1800 was about sixteen thousand) but weren't very profitable.

As early as 1730 Nantucket had twenty-five whalers. By 1840 there were over eighty Nantucket-owned brigs sailing around the world; there were five wharves in the harbor, thirty-six candle factories, rope "walks," sail lofts and shipyards. Almost everyone was connected with whaling—either going to sea directly or helping others to do so and waiting for their return. Because of their devotion to a single industry, these people became the most knowledgeable about whaling in the world. And this helps explain why Nantucket surpassed even the British in this livelihood who were their only serious competitors for many years. The British lacked the determination and energy (at least as far as whaling was concerned) and the courage which Nantucket men were forced to assume. Whaling was their only business whereas the British had commercial trade. The courage these people possessed is all but forgotten, most likely because we can't fully appreciate what they were up against. The basic equation was: a group of sailors plus harpoon plus eighteen-foot whale boat equals one whale (about a hundred feet or more in length). These animals were literally giants of the sea—among the largest animals in history. Their jaws were large enough and opened sufficiently wide to consume the entire whaling party and boat in one piece. And they were not known for their tranquility—especially when harpooned. The speed with which an angry whale could take the whalers for a "Nantucket sleigh ride" was frightening. Of greater concern was his diving or ramming either the whaleboat or the ship. In short, it was a risky and arduous profession.

The Early Years

In the beginning, there was nothing but the land and sea and Bartholomew Gosnold who accidentally discovered this "Far Away Island" in 1602—off course on his way to Virginia. The island was granted by King Charles I to the Earl of Sterling in 1635, who in turn six years later passed it on to his son, Thomas Mayhew, a Puritan merchant from Watertown, Mass. In 1659, a group of nine men together with friends and relatives purchased the island from Mayhew's son for thirty pounds and two beaver hats (they were very fashionable in those days and both Mayhew Junior and his wife had a need for one.) This was a bit more than was paid for the other island, Manhattan, thirty-five years before, but well worth the price. Nantucket, in fact, was originally a province of New York; the islanders sent a few barrels of fish each year to its Governor in lieu of taxes.

The original nine men included two Coffin brothers and Messrs. Folger, Macy, Swain, Hussey, Barnard, Greenleaf and Pike. They were all planters who lived in Salisbury, a community north of Boston. They wanted to escape the confines of the Puritan religion (which among other things upheld the union of Church and State) and therefore found the more permissive and simpler form of Quakerism so appealing. Thomas and Sarah Macy were among the first to arrive in the fall of 1659. They came by rowboat from Cape Cod and first settled at Madaket. By the next year there were over sixty settlers (including Tristram Coffin whose daughter, Mary Starbuck, was a leader in organizing the regular monthly meetings of Friends). The original settlement was to the southwest of present-day Nantucket town and was officially named Sherburne in 1673. It was not until 1795 that the name was officially changed to Nantucket.

It was about this time (1673) that shore whaling began. Obviously the supply was limited and gradually the farmers took to going out after the whales at greater and greater distances. By the turn of the century they were sailing around the Horn. The quest was for whale oil—primarily for England which consumed over four thousand tons of oil annually in homes and street lights. London was experiencing an epidemic of mugging at the time and therefore decided to keep the street lamps burning all night. Because of the close relationship between Nantucket and England, the former was granted a somewhat favorable status and, among other things, was exempted from the Massachusetts Restraining Bill of 1774 which restricted commerce elsewhere in New England.

In 1773 the "Dartmouth," the "Beaver" (owned by William Rotch, a prominent Nantucket merchant) and the "Eleanor"—all Nantucket ships—were chartered in London by the East India Company to deliver a cargo of tea to Boston. While the cargo was subsequently dumped overboard on arrival by "Indians," none of the ships was affected. But when the American war broke out, Nantucket was not in an enviable position. Because of her dependence on Britain, she could offer neither resistance nor support and, as a result, her vessels were destroyed by both sides, depending on which group had issued a sailing permit. They were at the mercy of both the British Navy and the American privateers and, for a short while, tried to substitute other businesses (including cod fishing) which appeared a bit safer. But these were not profitable endeavors; whaling was still the only answer. The hardship of the Revolutionary War marks the end of act one of our story.

Starting Over Again After The War

While most of her ships were destroyed in the war, those that were left and able to sail were the first to fly the flag of the new United States overseas—in England in 1783, in Quebec and various Spanish ports.

Gradually Nantucket men accumulated a great familiarity with the seas. For example, they were the first to have intimate knowledge of the Gulf Stream. When Captain Timothy Folger plotted it for Benjamin Franklin (who was Postmaster General at the time) in 1786, the sailing time to England was reduced by about two weeks. The British, considering themselves still the expert mariners, ignored the charts prepared by "those fishermen" and stuck to their traditional (and more lengthy) routes.

The end of act two of our story is climaxed with the War of 1812. By this time Nantucket had grown to a population of about seven thousand—including almost four hundred widows and as many fatherless children. Between the British blockade and the seizure of her vessels by both the British and French Navy (many Nantucket sailors were impressed into French service), life was pretty grim. Over half the whaling fleet was destroyed in the war and the island was thrown into a severe depression which lasted for over three years. But due to the characteristic faith and endurance of the islanders, by 1822 the island had tripled the size of its fleet and restored the whaling industry to its former level (while at the same time the British whaling business was floundering). This marks the beginning of the third and final act.

The Greatest Whaling Center in the World

Beginning in the 1820s and building up in the two succeeding decades, the Nantucket whaling economy grew rapidly. Herman Melville was struck by the courage and strength of the whalers who set forth alone from their little elbow of sand located away offshore. "And thus have these naked Nantucketers," as he described them in *Moby Dick,* "these sea-hermits, issuing from their anthill in the sea, overrun and conquered the watery world like so many Alexanders; parcelling out among them the Atlantic, Pacific, and Indian Oceans, as the three pirate powers did Poland. Let America add Mexico to Texas, and pile Cuba upon Canada; let the English overswarm all India, and hang out their blazing banner from the sun; two-thirds of this terraqueous globe are the Nantucketer's. For the sea is his; he owns it, as Emperors own empires; other seamen having but a right of way through it." As early as 1824 men like Captain George Chase were returning home with as much whale oil as England's entire annual consumption several years before. (Chase's haul was over three thousand barrels of oil after a three year voyage.) Eight years later (1832) over thirty whaling ships set out to sea in one year alone. By 1843 Nantucket had eighty-eight whalers out sailing around the world. But by this time the voyages were long and hard. The sailors' home was their ship and most of their time was spent in the forecastle, a rather dark and gloomy area "below." Food consisted of a mixture of tea, coffee and molasses, or another dish called "scouse," consisting of hard tack, beans and meat. Captain Benjamin Worth (*107*) spent forty-one years at sea, making thirty-four voyages in all. He is said to have sailed over a million miles, rounded the Horn sixteen times, brought in over nineteen thousand barrels of oil and never lost a man. The total amount of time he spent at home in forty-one years was about six years.

George W. Gardner went to sea at the age of thirteen for about the same number of years as Captain Worth. He was a master for half the period. Married at twenty-nine and father of fifteen children, he spent less than five years at home in the aggregate. In 1812, he was taken by the British and lost everything. In 1820, the "Essex" was rammed and sunk by an angry whale, forcing Captain George Pollard (*39*) and a handful of survivors to spend three months in an open lifeboat. This bleak story is thought to have been the basis for *Moby Dick*.

As the photographs in this book demonstrate, whaling for those who were fortunate and determined was rewarding. The Starbuck, Hadwen and Macy houses (*91, 93* and *97*) are excellent examples of the wealth that was accumulated from this single source. While the islanders were rather modest in their tastes, certain of them did enjoy such refinements as an upstairs ballroom with a sprung floor (it was easier on the feet) and a roof that opened to the stars (*92*) or maybe elaborate dinner parties—such as the William Crosbys gave at their One Pleasant Street home (*115*) where they introduced frozen mousse and other new dishes. Lower Main Street, formerly called State Street, was originally paved with cobblestones in 1837. These came over as ballast from the mainland (or America as it is commonly referred to by Nantucketers even today). While this was done for utilitarian purposes, enabling the heavy oil carts to move up from the wharves without sinking into the mud, the paving of upper Main Street in 1852 was for more aesthetic reasons. In addition, the great elm trees that line the street were planted by the Coffins about this time.

The good years in act three lasted only until the late 1840s. Then began the downfall, starting first with an enormous fire in 1846 which destroyed thirty-six acres of town buildings, homes, shops and most important, whale oil and related items stored in warehouses. In 1849 most of the better sailors decided prospecting for gold would be more profitable than for whale oil. A few years later, the Civil War siphoned off additional men. Beginning in the 1850s, the strip of sand known as the Nantucket Bar had blocked the harbor entrance to such extent that whalers could not cross even with the help of "camels"—specially designed cradles with pontoons that floated the ships high in the water. In 1854, a Waltham group began to produce petroleum oil commercially, the supply of which was guaranteed in 1859 when the first petroleum well was drilled in Pennsylvania. By 1869, Nantucket's last whalers set sail, and an era had ended.

Main Street Square

The Pacific Club (formerly the Rotch Market—1765) and fountain

The Pacific Bank (1818)

The vegetable girl—when she's off duty, you weigh your own

Fresh flowers of every kind and color are available each weekday morning.

31

Nothing is ever
out-of-date

Mitchell's
makes friends

The old blacksmith
shop (ca. 1855)

The Islanders still cherish their "gams."

The Atheneum (1847)

The Methodist Church (1823)

A Nantucket giftshop—originally the Capt. William Brock house (1760); also home of Capt. George Pollard of the "Essex"

The Whaling Museum (1847), originally William Hadwen's candle factory

The Peter Foulger Museum (1971)

Bicycles for hire, built for one or more

Our Lady of the Isle welcomes the
bicycles on Sunday morning

Fishing off Steamboat Wharf

Eating out . . . Nantucket style—the White Elephant

A Wall Street banker relaxing

Cliffside Beach Club

The Jetties and Cliffside "Beach Bug"

No attaché cases needed here

Playmates on Children's Beach

. . . Come again some other day

Life can't proceed without an ice
cream cone break.

A Harbor Square
gift shop

Sunday banking clients

Summer shopping

Swabbing down a lobster boat at sunrise

Back from sea

North Wharf houses, perched on stilts, overlook harbor activities.

The Wharf Rat Club: no seats reserved for the mighty; no by-laws, meetings or dues

Fishnets drying on a gray day

Early morning solitude.

The whalers are smaller now.

The start of a typical Nantucket day

The incomparable Old North Wharf . . . its houses . . . and lofts

Swain's Wharf

Old South Wharf

Harbor shore by
Commercial Wharf

The best way to get to Nantucket is to sail.

3
The Island Today

Today Nantucket still enjoys its insularity and pride. All digit dialing, cable television and jet plane service now connect it with America, but only on a temporary basis. All you have to do is visit the airport on a densely foggy Sunday afternoon—hearing the crowds cheer as each plane lands or takes off, as if a touchdown had been scored—to realize how isolated the island can really be. Anyone stuck overnight onboard the "Nantucket" anchored outside the jetties in the fog will certainly agree. Officially only a thirty-five minute jet flight from New York, the trip more often than not can take half a day—or longer, if bad weather lands you on the Vineyard or at Hyannis after the last boat.

But once you're there, it's like no other place. Over fifty-five miles of broad clean beaches encircle the small island. The water is often warmer than Long Island's south shore, thanks to the Gulf Stream. Crisscrossing the ten thousand acres of moors are miles of paths and unpaved roads taking the hiker through fields of heather, holly and scotch broom (*144* and *145*). The island is inhabited by deer, pheasant, quail and rabbits (by the thousands), but interestingly enough there are no squirrels or chipmunks. Scattered among the hills are fresh water ponds filled with perch and pickerel and surrounded by wintergreen, virginia creeper, and rugosa roses (*141, 142* and *143*). These ponds are the work of a glacier which originally formed Nantucket as a moraine that later became an island when rising waters filled the coastal plains. Offshore are bluefish and striped bass for the surf casters (*138* and *139*), especially at Madaket, as well as scallops for hardy souls in winter.

For those who find the lazy pace of Nantucket town too taxing, there's Madaket to the west and 'Sconset to the east. Quidnet was established as a refuge for the escapees from the urban ills of 'Sconset, and then there's Wauwinet—a community for those who would really prefer to be on a separate island but enjoy being connected with the rest of the world. Polpis, Quaise, Shimmo and Monomoy form little pockets of homes along the harbor shoreline like so many Greenwiches and Dariens—but this is no Fairfield County. This is sleepy Nantucket, one of the few entities in the country that's both town and county (not to mention an island). Tuckernuck and Muskeget, two privately owned islands which unfortunately are not open to visitors, and Esther, a newly formed island named after a hurricane, are all quietly anchored off Nantucket's west coast (*135, 164* to *167*). Tuckernuck was once nothing but farmland which was connected to Nantucket by a sandy road. Once upon a time and not so long ago, so the story goes, an elderly Coffin farmer drove his wagonload of produce into the town market and on his return that afternoon found that Tuckernuck had broken away. He eventually got home all right . . . by boat. Muskeget, on the other hand, has always been an island and therefore is less developed with houses and roads than its neighbor. The lonely building on the southern shore near the cove entrance was once a "humane house." (It is one of the oldest still standing. There are two others in this area, on Tuckernuck and at Madaket.) Manned by volunteers on rotating shifts, the humane houses launched rescue squads for ships endangered on Nantucket shoals and offered shelter for the shipwrecked.

There are three golf courses on the island which often present a unique handicap in the late afternoon (especially at Sankaty Head and 'Sconset) as the fog rolls across the fairways and play must be suspended until it temporarily lifts (184). On the way to either of these courses, you'll drive alongside one of the first bikeways built in this country. On a summer day it's busy with a wide assortment of cyclists and their machines—racers, lightweights, tandems, three wheelers for those who can't ride and occasionally a bicycle for three or four for those who don't know any better.

Lower Main Street is the scene of activity early on a summer morning, before beach time. Rows of Jeepsters and aging jalopies line both sides or form a circling parade as passengers spill out to pick up the paper or fresh flowers and vegetables (30 and 31). If the vegetable man is off to lunch, it doesn't matter—you simply weigh your own, figure out what you owe and deposit exact change in a box.

While waiting at "The Hub" for your Sunday paper, which often may not arrive until Monday evening, you'll notice an interesting collection of people: children with ice cream cones, Boston Brahmans in their worn out sneakers, and Nantucket women of all ages sporting lightship baskets. These baskets, once made during the long shifts at the lighthouses and lightships, are now the pride of Nantucket ladies, including the "regular" off-islanders. José Formoso Reyes, a native of the Philippines, still uses some of the original forms, although he has refined their design over the years (127). These baskets are equally at home at the A&P and the Yacht Club. They travel to the beach every day, are rained on and even occasionally sat on, and generally, under such "normal" conditions, they last forever.

By 9:00 p.m. the old Lisbon bell in South Tower (120) begins its sounding of the curfew as it has regularly done since 1849. Every evening it strikes fifty-two times—no one really knows why anymore but that doesn't matter since it's always been that way. And that's the story of Nantucket. Nothing ever changes much there, and no one really would want it to.

Sunrise and seagulls . . .

. . . and boats on the water

Reflections

New England's most beautiful harbor

The "Shenandoah"
at anchor

The Old Mill (1746) —originally called "Swain's Mill." Although crudely made by a mariner, it is well engineered and still operable.

Whether it's Wauwinet or New Zealand this compass shows the way.

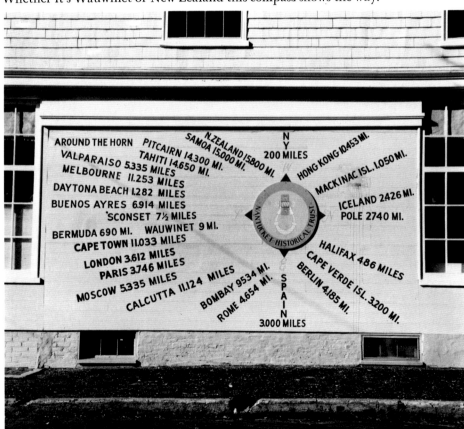

The Old Gaol (1805), one of the oldest in the United States. It is constructed of solid oak logs placed on top of one another and sheathed with iron on the inside. Offenders were held for indebtedness and embezzlement of funds.

4
Nantucket Architecture

A walk along upper Main Street offers an architectural happening unparalleled anywhere else in New England. When you consider that almost all of these houses are still in their original setting, unlike the more typical restored villages, the situation becomes that much more unique.

All of the homes on this street were built with whale oil. Most of the wealth was accumulated by the whale merchants and investors rather than the captains themselves. Zenas Coffin and Joseph Starbuck were two such men, and between them they account for thirteen of the most prominent Main Street residences. Zenas Coffin was one of the wealthiest men in America at the turn of the nineteenth century. His sons lived at Nos. 75 and 78 Main Street while his daughters occupied Nos. 90, 91 and 99 and granddaughters Nos. 86 and 98. Joseph Starbuck built three matching brick houses for his sons, Nos. 93, 95 and 97, while his daughters lived across the street at Nos. 92, 96 and 100.

The Macys were not to be outdone by such display. Francis, George, Silvanus, Thomas and Zaccheus all lived along the street (Nos. 77, 86, 89, 99 and 107 respectively), although it should be noted that Thomas married a Zenas Coffin girl and George a Zenas Coffin granddaughter.

The original Nantucket settlement was at Sherburne, between Capaum Pond and Hummock Pond. Capaum was open to the north shore at the time and afforded a protected harbor. When a storm closed it off in the latter part of the eighteenth century, the inhabitants gradually moved to a new site called Wesco, which is approximately where Nantucket is today. Because of the tremendous scarcity of wood, many houses were simply picked up and relocated; it was cheaper to move than to build. (In fact Herman Melville observed in *Moby Dick* that Nantucketers carried their wood around as if it were pieces of the true cross.)

The Elihu Coleman house, built in 1722 (*102*), is the only homestead remaining on its original site in Sherburne. The Christian house of 1720 (*105*) was moved into town in its entirety in 1741 by its owner Thomas Macy who then gave it to his son Nathaniel. Similarly the eastern section of the Christopher Starbuck house (*98*) is thought to have been built in Sherburne in 1690. The western half dates from around 1715. Sections of the Zaccheus Macy house (*99*) and the Joshua Coffin house (*107*) were also brought over from Sherburne.

Captain Richard Gardner's home, built in 1724 (*102*), is located on what used to be the main road between Sherburne and Wesco. Note the similarities in style between this and the Elihu Coleman house mentioned earlier. Both retain the central chimney originally incorporated in the houses of the mid to late seventeeth century. (See the Jethro Coffin house of 1686, pages *100* and *101*.) While the Coleman and Gardner houses have added second stories on the front, they still retain the steep shed roof to the north—facing south with their backs to the north wind.

The Jethro Coffin house has become known as the "Oldest House," although both "Shanunga" (*156*) and "Auld Lang Syne" (*157*) in 'Sconset are believed to predate it. This house was built as a wedding present for Jethro and his bride, Mary Gardner, by their respective fathers. The materials came from Peter Coffin's lumber lands and sawmill at Exeter, New Hampshire. The house was meant to be something special. The massive central chimney, large fireplaces, and lean-to style were characteristic of the time. So, too, was its "Indian closet" which might be considered a mid seventeenth-century bomb shelter, offering some protection during raids by the savages.

As the community moved eastward and began to settle at Wesco, the houses were located closer together and right on the street, in the English style. This is in contrast to other New England towns where houses often were set back behind lawns or gardens. As a result, Nantucket developed quickly into a city as opposed to a village. Even at the peak of whaling prosperity, Nantucketers preferred to build their stately homes right next to one another as they might have done in New York or Philadelphia. In fact Jared Coffin's wife was so unhappy about being stuck out at "Moor's End," completed in 1834 (*116* and *117*), that she convinced him to build a house closer to town, which he did in 1845 (*118* and *119*).

Proceeding up Main Street from the Pacific Bank, one notices two prominent homes, both of which were occupied by presidents of the bank. No. 72 Main Street (*82*) was built by John Wendall Barrett in 1820. This dignified house barely survived the Great Fire of 1846, not because the flames were about to engulf it but because the firewards intended to blow it up to check the fire's spread. Mrs. Barrett simply refused to leave and fortunately the direction of the fire changed, sparing the house. Frederick Mitchell built the house opposite at 69 Main Street (*84*) in 1834. He was a whaling merchant and also was president of the bank.

Henry and Charles Coffin, sons of Zenas Coffin, built the identical

houses at 78 and 75 Main Street between 1831 and 1833 (*85* and *86*).
Charles was a Quaker and preferred the conservative brownstone trim,
whereas Henry had white trim and a cupola instead of an exposed roof
walk. The two brothers were quite philanthropic, planting the elm trees
on Main Street in 1851 and bringing a wide variety of wildlife to the
island at about the same time (including over forty thousand English
pine trees).

The rooftop walk, like the one on the Sidney Chase House at 82
Main Street (*86*), was an essential part of Nantucket architecture, enabling the women to watch for the return of their sailing husbands.
They have often been called "widows' walks" which is a mistake because clearly if a woman were indeed a widow she would have no need
to be up there. George Macy lived at 86 Main Street (*87*) in a house
built by his wife's grandfather, Zenas Coffin, in 1834. His uncle, Matthew Crosby, a successful whaler and subsequent ship owner and merchant, lived in the Federalist house at 90 Main Street (*88*), which was
built in 1829. Note the similarity between this and Thomas Macy II's
house at 99 Main Street, built two years before in 1827 (*97*). Both
Crosby and Macy married Zenas Coffin girls. Captain Job Coleman
lived at 88 Main Street (*87*), a home which dates from about 1830. He
was one of the first to sail for California in 1849 at the beginning of the
famous rush for gold.

Across the street are two houses dating from the early 1800s (*91*).
Silvanus Macy, a prominent whale fitter and brother of Obed Macy
(*106*), lived at No. 89, the original portion of which dates from 1740,
while Henry Swift and his bride (another Zenas Coffin girl) lived hap-
pily at No. 91.

The three identical houses located at Nos. 93, 95 and 97 Main
Street (*91* and *93*) are commonly referred to as "The Three Bricks."
They were built between 1836 and 1838 by Joseph Starbuck for his
three sons, William, Matthew and George. He also built a whaler named
for those sons, the "Three Brothers," which returned in 1859 with six
thousand barrels of oil after a voyage of almost five years, both of these
feats being records. Matthew's house, the "Middle Brick," still remains
in the family. Joseph Starbuck's daughters lived directly opposite the
"Three Bricks" at Nos. 92, 96 and 100. The first of these houses was
built in 1838 by William Swain. The second, along with its companion
next door (No. 94), was constructed between 1840 and 1845 by
William Hawden, a silversmith, whale oil merchant and a candle maker

(*92* and *93*). The refined Greek style of these houses, which were designed by Frederick Brown Coleman, represents the zenith of whaling prosperity. No. 94 has a second floor ballroom with a specially sprung dance floor and a rooftop dome that can be opened to the stars. William Hadwen and his partner, Nathaniel Barney, originally lived in a two family house at No. 100 (*94*), the rear portion of which dates from the early 1700s. This home was later occupied by Joseph Mitchell who was a whaler, a " '49er" and a president of the Pacific Bank. Hadwen also built and operated, with Barney, the brick candle factory now housing the Whaling Museum (*39*). In between the two Hadwen homes lived Jared Coffin's son, Benjamin, who like his father was also a whale oil merchant. This dignified house was built in 1836 (*94*) and has an accompanying sidewalk paved with bluestone. The James Bunker house at No. 102 (*96*) is believed to be one of the first houses in Nantucket built of two stories from front to back. It dates from about 1740.

Zaccheus Macy, grandson of Thomas Macy, one of the island's first settlers, lived in the house at 107 Main Street (*99*), thought to have been built in 1748. Zaccheus was a prominent whaler and boat builder. On the side he was an expert setter of broken bones, having studied the subject extensively in his youth. It is estimated that he set about two thousand bones during his lifetime (all for free). Reuben Joy, for whom the homestead is presently named, was its subsequent owner. He was also a whaling captain.

The Peter Folger II House on Center Street (*103*), built in 1750, was occupied by Folgers for almost two hundred years. Peter I was a grandfather of Benjamin Franklin. The unusual third story was added in 1815.

The second story design of Job Macy's house, also completed in 1750 (*105*), was such a radical departure from the accepted lean-to look that his father, a strict Quaker, vowed never to enter it. And he kept his word. Around the corner at 15 Pleasant Street lived Nantucket's first historian, Obed Macy (*106*). He was also a ship fitter and builder, in partnership with his brother, Sylvanus. There were three generations of Macy partnerships in this business, continuing with their respective sons, Thomas and Peter, and grandsons Isaac and Philip. Another grandson of Sylvanus (and grandnephew of Obed) was Rowland H. Macy who started a dry goods business in New York.

Maria Mitchell was born in the house on Vestal Street subsequently named for her (*108*). It was built in 1790. Her father never attended college but nevertheless was an overseer of Harvard (the standards were lower in those days). He was also a cashier at the Pacific Bank on whose roof she had her observatory. Maria became one of our foremost astronomers and was a professor at Vassar.

While Orange Street (*113*) boasted the reputation of being home to a hundred and twenty-six whaling captains, it was Pleasant Street that rivaled Main Street for expression of whaling wealth. John Coleman designed the two graceful homes at Nos. 7 and 9 during the early 1820s (*114* and *115*). His brother, Frederick, designed the Greek revival mansions on Main Street about twenty years later, as well as the Baptist and Methodist Churches and the Atheneum, which was probably his greatest achievement (*36, 37* and *121*). Both architects were noted for their excellent taste, proportionate designs, and their carving and finishing skills. They were two of the most influential men to shape the face of Nantucket. William Crosby and his wife lived at One Pleasant Street (*115*), a home which was completed in 1837. It became known as Nantucket's "social center" with the Crosbys entertaining regularly. The house was decorated with marble mantle pieces, French doors and silver doorknobs.

"Moor's End" was built between 1829 and 1834 by Jared Coffin (*116* and *117*) who had accumulated a fortune through partnerships in three successful whaleships. As previously mentioned, Mrs. Coffin felt it was too far out of town and convinced him to build another home in town in 1845 (*118* and *119*). A year later they packed up and moved to Boston, again most likely at her request. "Moor's End" was sold and resold many times. Finally in 1873 it was put up for auction and Jared Gardner bought it for $2,350. (He also bought the Old Mill in 1822 for twenty dollars and was going to use it for firewood but later changed his mind when he saw how difficult it would be to take apart.) "Moor's End" is probably the island's most beautiful home, and it was practically given away—an indication of the extreme poverty which had befallen the island at that time. While the values of this and other fine homes were unusually depressed in the 1870s, it is interesting to note how inflated they have become exactly one hundred years later!

This brief commentary and accompanying photographs focus on a few of the more interesting and important Nantucket residences from the whaling era. There are many more that unfortunately have had to be omitted but they are all still there for the visitor to see.

The John Wendell Barrett house, 72 Main Street (1820)

The front stoop of the Barrett house

The Francis Macy house, 77 Main Street (1790; 1836)

The Charles Coffin
house, 78 Main Street
(1831)

The Frederick Mitch-
ell house, 69 Main
Street (1834)

The Charles Coffin house

The Sidney Chase house, 82 Main Street (1820)

The Henry Coffin house, 75 Main Street (1833)

The George Macy house, 86 Main Street (1834)
The Job Coleman house, 88 Main Street (ca. 1830) and
The Matthew Crosby house, 90 Main Street (1829)

The Matthew Crosby house, 90 Main Street (1829)

Looking up Main Street past the Job Coleman house

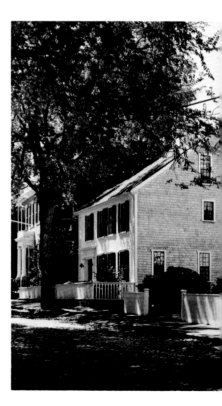

The "Three Bricks," at 93, 95 and 97 Main Street (1836-1838)

The Henry Swift house, 91 Main Street (ca. 1820) and
The Silvanus Macy house, 89 Main Street (1740; 1800)

No. 94 Main Street

Left, The "East Brick"

Right, The William Hadwen houses
94 and 96 Main Street (1840-1845)

The "Hadwen-Satler Memorial,"
96 Main Street

The Benjamin Coffin house, 98 Main Street (1836)

The Joseph Mitchell house, 100 Main Street (ca. 1730; 1810)

Main Street cobble-stones

A sign of Nantucket friendship

The James Bunker house, 102 Main Street
(ca. 1740)

The Thomas Macy II house, 99 Main Street (1770; 1827)

The Christopher Starbuck house, 105 Main Street (1690; 1753)

The Richard Gardner
house, 139 Main Street (ca.
1686)

The Zaccheus Macy house
("The Reuben Joy Home-
stead"), 107 Main Street
(1748)

The Jethro Coffin house ("The Oldest House") (1686)

The Elihu Coleman
house in Sherburne
(1722)

The Richard Gardner
III house, 32 West
Chester Street (1724)

The Peter Folger II house,
51 Center Street (1750)

Early houses on Vestal Street

The Nathanial Macy house (also the Christian house) on Walnut Lane (1720)

Mill Street and New Dollar Lane, the Job Macy house (1750) and an early 19th century companion

A Coffin house on Lilly Street

The Obed Macy house, 15 Pleasant Street (1800)

The home of Benjamin
Worth, 26 Liberty Street, who
spent forty-one years at sea and
a total of six at home between
voyages

The Joshua Coffin house, 52
Center Street (1756)

The Hezekiah Swain house (also the Maria Mitchell house), One Vestal Street (1790)

The Woodbox Inn, 29 Fair Street (ca. 1740)

Gray cedar shingles give the houses a mellowed look.

The Matthew Myrick house, 6 Prospect Street (ca. 1740)

A flag and flower boxes are standard equipment in Nantucket. The Tristram Starbuck house, 12 Milk Street (1784)

The Thomas Coffin house (also the Hinchman house), 7 Milk Street (1810)

Looking down Orange Street—once the home of 126 whaling captains

The John Coleman homes, 9 and 7 Pleasant Street (1821-1824)

The William Crosby house, One Pleasant Street (1837)

The Benjamin Easton house, 9 Pleasant Street (1824)

"Moor's End" built by Jared Coffin, 19 Pleasant Street (1829-1834)

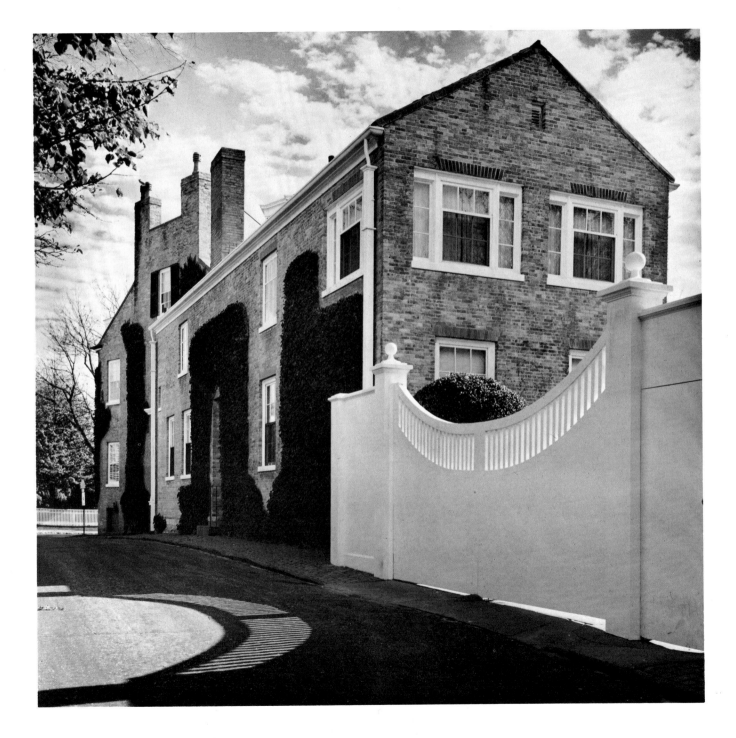

Coffin house, 29 Broad Street (1845)

Old South Church (also "Second Congregational" and eventually "Unitarian") on Fair Street (1809)

The First Baptist Church (1840)

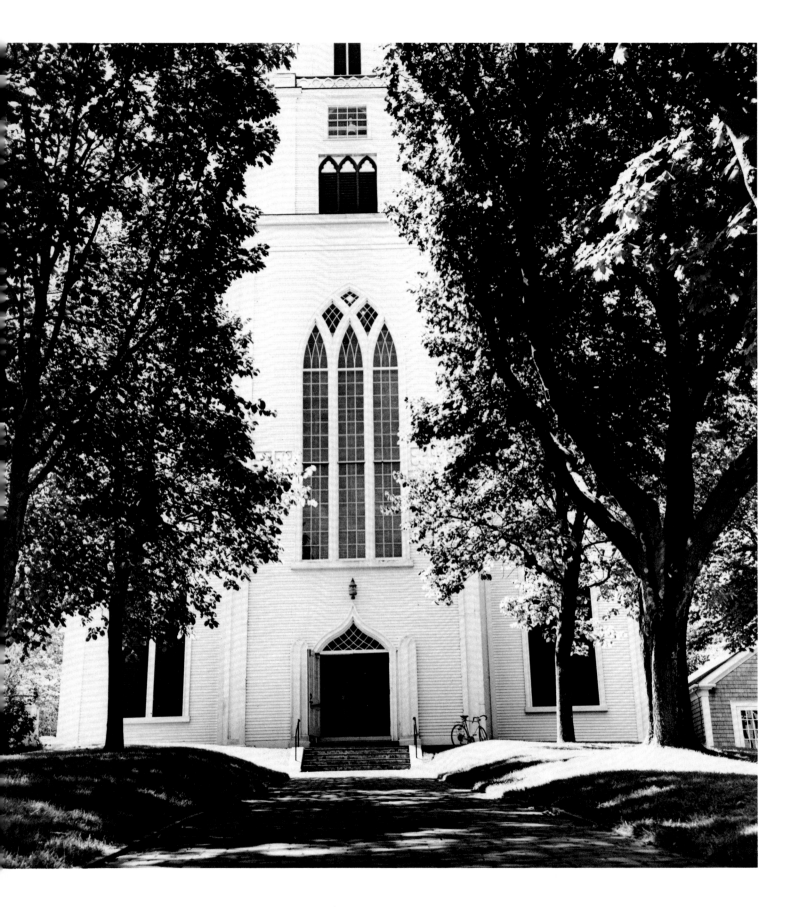

Old North Church (or "First Congregational") on Center Street (1834)

Gull Island Lane

The Old North Cemetery

A typical landscape—water is never far away

Mr. Reyes and his lightship baskets

Madaket anglers

Crabbing

Beach path

Sand dunes at Great Point

A deserted beach on Esther Island

Hummock Pond was once open to the sea near Cisco.

Cisco Beach

Over fifty-five miles of clean sandy beach encircle the island.

Madaket

Ducks on a Polpis pond

A secluded pond in Quaise surrounded by bayberry, holly and bearberry

Wintergreen, bayberry and holly by Gibbs Pond. John Gibbs (Assassamoogh) was a Nantucket Indian, a minister, and a Harvard graduate.

Gibb's Pond

Maxcy's Pond

Over 10,000 acres of moors—rich with Scotch broom, heather, beach plum, bayberry and holly

The view from Altar Rock on Macy Hill, about 90 feet above sea level

Swamp maples, beeches, tupelos and a carpet of ferns in the Hidden Forest

The Pine Forest off the 'Sconset Road

The Hidden Forest in Polpis

The Bridge at 'Sconset (1887) and sun dial—it's 12:00 noon, EST

5
Siasconset

There's a little village with the distinction of being situated furthest out in the Atlantic Ocean, and with good reason; it illustrates how much its original inhabitants wanted to get away from the rest of the world. Such is the place called 'Sconset. This community and another similar one to the north, Sesachacha, were among the first settlements on the island (about 1675). In fact, Mitchell Coffin's "Auld Lang Syne" (*157*) is thought to have been built in that year and therefore would be eleven years senior to Jethro Coffin's "Oldest House."

The cluster of houses along 'Sconset's east bank had a modest beginning as one room fishing shacks. All cooking was done outside and the overall spartan, camp-like atmosphere was appealing to the men. Eventually their women began to drive out from Nantucket town to visit and were also drawn to its simplicity. But to live there required some sprucing up of the rustic fishing cabins. The first round of additions were "warts," tiny bedrooms added to one side of the house which at first blush appeared minute but in actuality were more spacious than the average ship's cabin.

Next came a room on the opposite side of the house which was called a "porch" but in reality was the kitchen. All of these modest homes were constructed out of secondhand items. Lumber, doors and windows were carted out from town and assembled in a great mixture of materials. One wart on the "Martin Box" (*157*) was originally an old boat house, while the northern wing of the John Morris house (*153*) began life as a hay shed.

At the same time the mainland was celebrating its independence from England, 'Sconset was celebrating its liberation from the rain barrels—with the drilling of its first well in 1776 (*155*). With this the village began to thrive. By the 1830s and 1840s, it was a popular spot for whaling captains and their crew to visit when they were home from a voyage. It offered a needed respite from the unfamiliar bustle of life in town.

Gradually 'Sconset became Nantucket's Newport. Large fashionable summer houses were built for the townspeople who wanted to get away for a while. They preferred a more spacious and stately style of home to the dwarf fishing shacks. This was just fine with the theatrical set who subsequently began to discover the little "doll houses" and who were enchanted with the idea of crawling in and out of doorways and bending down to clean out the wart gutters.

The story of 'Sconset is one of isolation and quiet retreat. While

Nantucket has gone through various stages of growth and prosperity, the simplicity and solitude of 'Sconset has remained essentially the same throughout—interrupted only on occasion, such as when the young David Sarnoff and his colleagues were operating the first wireless station in the country here in the early 1900s. (He subsequently retired from this job and established R. C. A.)

As for the fate of neighboring Sesachacha, which was settled at the same time as 'Sconset and at one point was a larger village, no one really knows. It was just that much further to get to and gradually the towns-people preferred to cluster around 'Sconset. Some of the houses were moved down and the rest were abandoned. "Shanunga" (156), whose oldest section dates from 1682, was originally a Sesachacha fishing cottage. (At various times this house has been a store, an inn and tavern, and even the village post office, beginning in 1873.)

Much has been written about 'Sconset over the years as indeed has been Nantucket. But while the historians have dwelt on the latter, 'Sconset has been the province of the poets. The little poem by Bliss Carmen is among the best known and sums it up pretty well:

"Did you ever hear of 'Sconset where there's nothing
much but moors,
And beach and sea and silence and eternal out-of-doors—
Where the azure round of ocean meets the paler dome of day,
Where the sailing clouds of summer on the sea line melt away,
And there's not an ounce of trouble
Anywhere?
Where the field-larks in the morning will be crying at the door,
With the whisper of the moor-wind and the surf along the shore;
Where the little shingled houses down the little grassy street
Are grey with salt of sea-winds, and the strong sea-air is sweet
With the flowers in their door-yards;
Me for there!"

" 'Sconset" by Bliss Carmen

The John C. Morris house

Downtown 'Sconset

The 'Sconset Pump (1776) and Post Office

"Shanunga" (1682) also called the Betsy Cary House

"Nauticon Lodge" (1734)

"Martin Box" (1720)

"Auld Lang Syne" (1675) — the oldest house on Nantucket

"Snug Harbor" (1780)

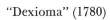
"Dexioma" (1780)

The George Gardner house (1740)

"Hearts Ease" (1815)

"Castle Bandbox" (1814)

"The Maples" (1800)

"Ivy Lodge" (1780)

The "Chanticleer"

Lisbon is the next town East.

A 'Sconset tandem

East Bank houses in 'Sconset

Welcome to Wauwinet.

The Wauwinet Casino

Wauwinet

Quidnet

Coskata Beach

"Madaket Millie's"

A "Crooked House" in Madaket

Madaket

The "humane house" on Muskeget Island

Tuckernuck's beautiful south shore

Tuckernuck Island—once a farming community and now just a quiet but private retreat

Feeding the Gulls

Sankaty golf course

Sankaty Head Lighthouse (1848)

Great Point Lighthouse (1818)

Heading back home

The seven o'clock boat

Come again soon

Acknowledgements

Edouard A. Stackpole,

Harry Amdur, Peter C. Bunnel,
James Lentowski, Samuel S. Walker, Jr.,

Charles M. Antin, Susan Banker, Martin Cook,
Douglas C. Fonda, Jr., Mimi Foster, Alan Frese,
Walter Frese, Christopher Harris, Susan T. Hill,
John V. Hinshaw, John Kittila, Morgan Levine,
Martha and Robert Strain, Dorothy and Robert Tonkin,
Leroy H. True, Dick Williams (pages 16, 17, 20, 51, 137),
Phoebe Dunn (pages 45, 46, 138, 139), Gene Mahon (135),
Nantucket Photo Shop, Quintessence Studio,
The Nantucket Conservation Foundation, Inc.,
The Nantucket Historical Association,
The Nantucket Historical Trust,
The Whaling and Marine Manuscript Archives, Inc.

Benchley, Peter, "Life's Tempo on Nantucket." *National Geographic,* Vol. 137, No. 6 (June, 1970).

Coffin, Patricia, *Nantucket.* New York: Viking Press, Inc., 1971.

Forman, Henry Chandlee, ed., *Underhill's Old Houses on 'Sconset Bank.* Nantucket: Myacomet Press, 1961.
> Based on a series of articles by Edward F. Underhill which appeared in the " 'Sconset Pump" in 1888.

Guba, Emil F., *Nantucket Odyssey.* Waltham, Mass.: published by the author, 1965.

Lancaster, Clay, *The Architecture of Historic Nantucket.* New York: McGraw-Hill, Inc., 1972.

Macy, Obed, *History of Nantucket.* Boston: Hilliard Gray & Co., 1835.

Stackpole, Edouard A., *Rambling through the Streets and Lanes of Nantucket.* Nantucket: published by the author, 1947.

Starbuck, Alexander, *History of Nantucket; County Island and Town.* Boston: C. E. Goodspeed & Co., 1924.

" 'Sconset" from *Echoes from Vagabondia* by Bliss Carmen, reprinted by permission from Dodd, Mead & Company, New York.